SKY HIGH
SOUTH DEVON COAST

PHOTOGRAPHY BY JASON HAWKES

First published in Great Britain in 2009

Photographs © 2009 Jason Hawkes

All rights reserved. No part of this publication may be reproduced, stored in a retrieval system, or transmitted in any form or by any means without the prior permission of the copyright holder.

British Library Cataloguing-in-Publication Data
A CIP record for this title is available from the British Library

ISBN 978 1 906887 51 3

PiXZ Books
Halsgrove House, Ryelands Industrial Estate,
Bagley Road, Wellington, Somerset TA21 9PZ
Tel: 01823 653777
Fax: 01823 216796
email: sales@halsgrove.com

An imprint of Halstar Ltd, part of the Halsgrove group of companies
Information on all Halsgrove titles is available at: www.halsgrove.com

Printed and bound by Grafiche Flaminia, Italy

Introduction

In this book we are taken on an aerial journey along the South Devon coast starting at Plymouth and heading east for some 115 miles (184km) where we reach the Dorset border. The coast is famous for its safe harbours around which, from ancient times, little communities established themselves. It is towards this shore that most of Devon's rivers run, creating deep tidal valleys. Some of the most desirable and expensive homes in Britain are to be found here. And where fishing boats once tied up alongside granite harbour walls, yachts now lay up at pontoons or rock gently at vast marinas.

The South Devon coastline provides the means for thousands to enjoy leisure pursuits. The South West Coast Path follows the cliff edge for most of its route through South Devon, while sandy beaches are thronged in summer months providing safe bathing in most places, while easy access provides a chance to explore harbourside towns and villages.

Jason Hawkes is one of the country's best-known photographers specialising in aerial photography, and this little book is the perfect memento for those who wish to take a little bit of Devon home with them.

Plymouth Hoe with the city of Plymouth stretching beyond.

At the mouth of the River Yealm, with Wembury seen on the left.

Left: The Cattewater and the River Plym.

One of Devon's most picturesque locations; Newton Ferrers on the River Yealm.

Where the River Erme enters the sea.

Famous Burgh Island faces Bigbury on the mainland.

The village of Thurlestone.

Right: Hope Cove, around which lie the villages of Outer and Inner Hope.

A scattering of boats on the shore at Hope Cove.

Overleaf:
South Sands, at the mouth of Salcombe harbour.

A busy beach scene near East Portlemouth.

Left: A view towards Salcombe with Bolt Head far distant.

A view westward down the Devon coast with the village of East Prawle visible far right.

A magnificent view into the South Hams, with East Prawle on the left.

The most southerly point in Britain, Start Point.

Slapton Ley is the largest freshwater lake in the South West and an important nature reserve.

Left: In 1917 the village of Hallsands was lost to the sea. Now only ruins remain.

At the mouth of the River Dart.

Right: Dartmouth.

Dartmouth Royal Naval College was built in the early 1900s.

Right: Kingswear lies on the River Dart, opposite Dartmouth.

The sweep of Brixham harbour extends into the heart of Tor Bay.

Roundham Head and Paignton harbour.

Left: Brixham harbour and town.

The Pier and Esplanade at Paignton.

Torquay harbour.

Oddicombe Beach, below St Marychurch.

Left: The former elegance of Torquay survives in the sweep of Hesketh Terrace.

A stunning view up the River Teign, with Teignmouth right and Shaldon on the left.

This sand spit creates a natural harbour at Teignmouth.

Shaldon.

Overleaf:
Beach huts at Teignmouth.

Dawlish.

Right: The mouth of the River Exe looking inland towards Exeter, Exmouth on the right.

The Esplanade and seafront at Exmouth.

Left: Topsham lies on the River Exe between Exmouth and Exeter.

Looking down on to Exmouth, with cricket being played on the Maer.

The distinctive red cliffs sweep eastward towards Sandy Bay.

The Royal Marines firing range at Sandy Bay.

Left: Sandy Bay holiday park dominates the coastline.

Budleigh Salterton looking west.

Left: Looking east over Budleigh Salterton, the River Otter entering the sea far right.

Sunny summer weather at Sidmouth.

Left: The view westward from above Budleigh Salterton.

The Esplanade, Sidmouth.

East towards Beer, with Seaton far distant.

Left: The view west from above Branscombe. The wreck of the *Napoli* lies offshore.

The village centre, Beer.

The view over Seaton. The River Axe forms the county boundary between Devon and Dorset.

Right: Offshore fun.

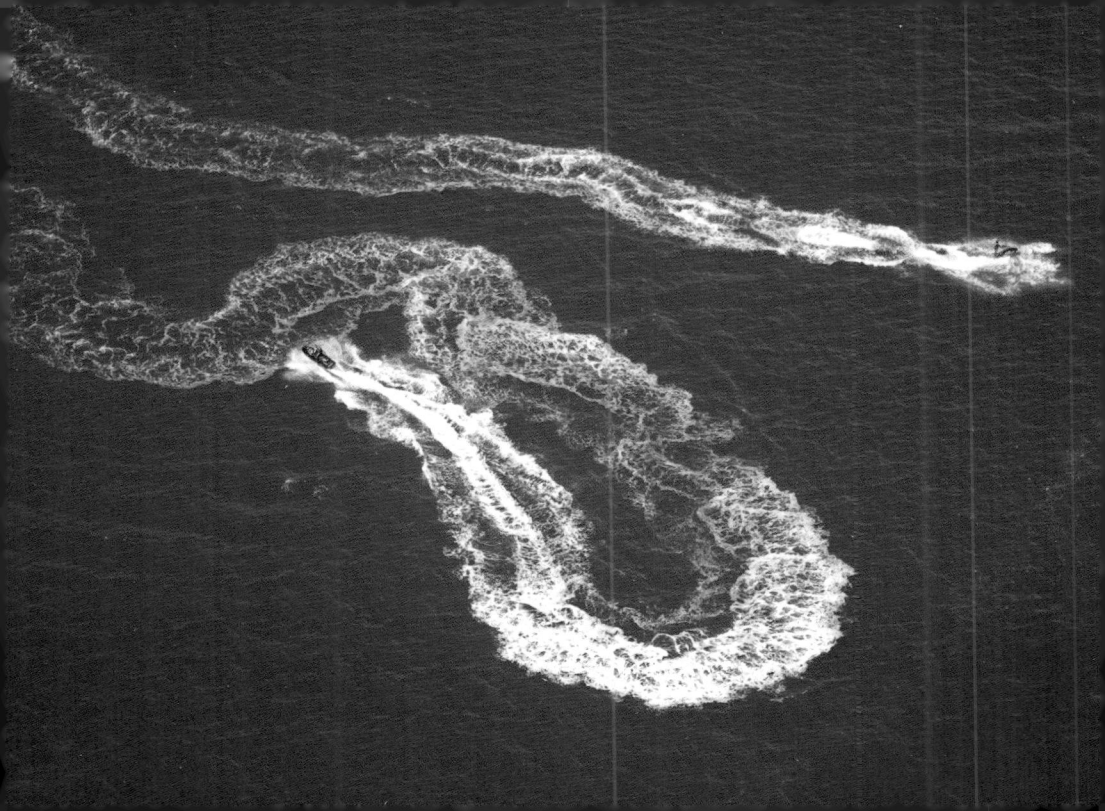

The last of Devon. Westwards down the coast towards Seaton.